Daily *warm-ups*

TEST-PREP WORDS

J. WESTON
WALCH
PUBLISHER
Portland, Maine

Purchasers of this book are granted the right to reproduce all pages. This permission is limited to a single teacher, for classroom use only.

Any questions regarding this policy or requests to purchase further reproduction rights should be addressed to:

Permissions Editor
J. Weston Walch, Publisher
321 Valley Street • P.O. Box 658
Portland, Maine 04104-0658

Certified Chain of Custody
Promoting Sustainable
Forest Management
www.sfiprogram.org

SGS-SFI/COC-US09/5501

1   2   3   4   5   6   7   8   9   10

ISBN 0-8251-4484-1

The *Daily Warm-Ups* series is a wonderful way to turn extra classroom minutes into valuable learning time. The 180 quick activities—one for each day of the school year—review, practice, and teach words that are commonly included on standardized tests such as the SAT. These daily activities may be used at the very beginning of class to get students into learning mode, near the end of class to make good educational use of that transitional time, in the middle of class to shift gears between lessons—or whenever else you have minutes that now go unused.

Daily Warm-Ups are easy-to-use reproducibles—simply photocopy the day's activity and distribute it. Or make a transparency of the activity and project it on the board. You may want to use the activities for extra-credit points or as a check on critical-thinking skills and problem-solving skills.

However you choose to use them, *Daily Warm-Ups* are a convenient and useful supplement to your regular lesson plans. Make every minute of your class time count!

altercation (n)—a noisy dispute

From Latin *altercare* (to wrangle)

The **altercation** between the two teams erupted after the umpire made several bad calls.

_____

Think of three synonyms for *altercation*. Write them below.

_____   _____   _____

Now use *altercation* and two of its synonyms in sentences of your own.

opulent (adj)—demonstrating great wealth; extravagant

From Latin *ops* (power, help)

The **opulent** lifestyle of the business tycoon was evident in his luxurious mansion on the ocean.

_____

Think of three antonyms for *opulent*. Write them below.

_____   _____   _____

Now think of three items that might be part of an opulent lifestyle. Write them below.

2

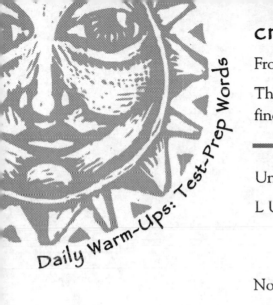

cryptic (adj)—secret; mysterious

From Greek *kryptos*

The **cryptic** message was read and reread by the detective trying to find the missing child.

_____

Unscramble the following letters to discover a synonym for *cryptic*.

L U C T O C _____

Now use *cryptic* in a sentence of your own.

fiasco (n)—a failure

From Italian *fiasco* (a flask or bottle)

This word is associated with bottles because glassblowers, in learning to blow glass properly, made many mistakes and ended up with badly misshapen bottles.

We hoped the school play would be a great success, but it turned out to be a **fiasco.**

_____

Write three synonyms for *fiasco*.

_____   _____   _____

Now use *fiasco* in a sentence of your own.

4

nocturnal (adj)—pertaining to the night; active at night

From Latin *nox* (night)

Owls are **nocturnal** animals.

What is the opposite of *nocturnal*? _____

Use both *nocturnal* and its opposite in one sentence.

whet (vb)—to sharpen; to stimulate

From German *waz* (sharp)

My brief trip to Europe served to **whet** my appetite for more travel.

Write two examples of things that can be whetted besides your appetite.

_____   _____

Now use *whet* in a sentence of your own.

intrepid (adj)—fearless; bold

From Latin *in* (not) and *trepidus* (trembling; alarmed)

In spite of poor visibility, the **intrepid** explorer continued his climb up the snow-covered mountain.

Write some synonyms and antonyms for *intrepid*.

Synonyms   **Antonyms**

demagogue (n)—a leader who promises things to people to gain power

From Greek *demos* (people) and *agogos* (leader)

After the election, the **demagogue**'s supporters were disappointed when he did not fulfill his campaign promise.

_____

Can you think of another word that contains the root *demo*?

Write it here. _____

Now use *demagogue* in a sentence of your own.

8

superfluous (adj)—beyond what is necessary; excessive

The speaker's explanation of the process was **superfluous;** the audience already understood the objective.

Decide whether each word below is a synomym or an antonym of *superfluous*. Write each word under the appropriate heading.

extra   inessential   bare   wasteful   necessary
minimal   extravagant   surplus   sparse   scanty

Synonyms   **Antonyms**

emulate (vb)—to try to equal by imitating

Many kids try to **emulate** their favorite movie stars by copying their fashions.

Circle the letter of the pair of words that is related in the same way as the pair in capital letters.

EMULATE : COPY ::

(A) praise : embarrass

(B) challenge : complete

(C) repair : mend

(D) divert : focus

(E) ignite : extinguish

Now use *emulate* in a sentence of your own.

10

assiduous (adj)—hard-working; diligent

She was not a natural athlete, but with **assiduous** effort she became the best soccer player at the school.

_____

Write three synonyms for *assiduous*.

_____   _____   _____

Now use *assiduous* in a sentence of your own.

conform (vb) — to become similar; to act in agreement

In order to **conform** to the stated school dress code, all young men had to wear ties.

Choose the word that is most closely related in meaning to *conform*.

(A) challenge (B) reward (C) agree (D) disagree

Now choose the word that is most nearly opposite in meaning.

(A) obey (B) affirm (C) omit (D) differ

Now use *conform* in a sentence of your own.

12

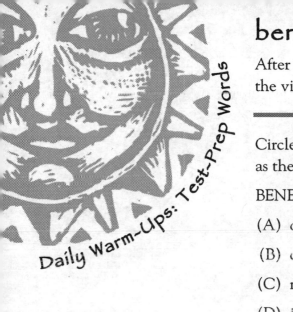

benevolent (adj)—kindly; charitable

After the earthquake, many **benevolent** volunteer groups assisted the victims.

Circle the letter of the pair of words that is related in the same way as the pair in capital letters.

BENEVOLENT : DONOR ::

(A) quiet : orator

(B) disloyal : competitor

(C) nimble : athlete

(D) inquisitive : researcher

(E) honorable : traitor

Now use *benevolent* in a sentence of your own.

13

spurious (adj)—fake; false; counterfeit

The political candidate's **spurious** claims misled people into thinking he had accomplished much in his short time in office.

Decide whether each word below is a synonym or an antonym of *spurious*. Write each word under the appropriate heading.

valid   factual   fraudulent   phony   affected   genuine

Synonyms   **Antonyms**

14

Now use *spurious* in a sentence of your own.

precocious (adj)—brilliant or expert at an early age

The **precocious** child was able to speak several foreign languages by the time she was eight.

Choose the word that is most closely related in meaning to *precocious*.

(A) special   (B) precious   (C) talkative   (D) gifted

Write two antonyms of *precocious*.

_____

Now use *precocious* in a sentence of your own.

infer (vb)—to conclude; to deduce

From the teacher's frown, the students **inferred** that they had not done well on the state test.

Sometimes you are asked to draw inferences from your reading. What does *inference* mean in this context?

Now use *infer* in a sentence of your own.

16

inevitable (adj)—unavoidable

Once the intense marketing campaign was launched, it was **inevitable** that the product would be a best-seller.

_____

Write two antonyms for *inevitable*.

_____   _____

Write one sentence using both *inevitable* and one of its antonyms.

_____

17

hedonist (n)—a pleasure seeker

Hedonism is the doctrine that happiness or pleasure is the chief good in life.

The **hedonist** did not care about the poverty that surrounded the resort.

Describe what you imagine the lifestyle of a hedonist to be.

18

Now use *hedonist* in a sentence of your own.

abbreviate (vb)—to shorten; to abridge

The teacher asked us to **abbreviate** all the names of states rather than write them out.

Circle the antonym of *abbreviate*:   reduce   lengthen   truncate

Now use *abbreviate* in a sentence of your own.

19

condescending (adj)—patronizing

The hostess's **condescending** look and tone of voice caused us to leave the restaurant.

━━━━━━━━━━━━━━━━━━━━━━━━━━━━━

Write two synonyms for *condescending*.

_____   _____

Can you think of an antonym for *condescending*? Write it here.

_____

Now use *condescending* in a sentence of your own.

20

florid (adj)—flushed; ornate

The **florid** writing style of the author was in sharp contrast to the spare, concise writing of the editor.

Circle the letter of the pair of words that is related in the same way as the pair in capital letters.

FLORID : ORNATE ::

(A) facile : difficult

(B) impulsive : unpredictable

(C) extraneous : irrelevant

(D) simple : complex

(E) gregarious : cautious

Now use *florid* in a sentence of your own.

21

© 2003 J. Weston Walch, Publisher

rancor (n)—hatred

Rancor filled every sentence of every exchange between the two political candidates throughout the debate.

_____

Write one synonym and one antonym for *rancor*.

Synonym: _____

Antonym: _____

Now use *rancor* in a sentence of your own.

22

venerable (adj)—respectable because of age

The family's **venerable** matriarch spoke to throngs of admirers at her one-hundredth-birthday party.

_____

Complete the following analogy:

venerable : person :: antique : _____

Now use *venerable* in a sentence of your own.

23

prosaic (adj)—dull; ordinary; run-of-the-mill

The student's **prosaic** writing style bored her literature teacher so much that he disliked grading her essays.

_____

Write an antonym for *prosaic:* _____

Now use *prosaic* in a sentence of your own.

24

impetuous (adj)—acting suddenly with little thought

The **impetuous** stockbroker sold off his holdings as soon as the market dipped slightly.

Give three examples of impetuous behavior or actions.

_____

_____

_____

Now use *impetuous* in a sentence of your own.

25

© 2003 J. Weston Walch, Publisher

sagacious (adj)—shrewd

John prides himself on being a **sagacious** judge of character, but his brother has difficulty understanding people.

Circle the word that does not belong with the others.

intelligent   astute   sharp   witless   ingenious

Now use *sagacious* in a sentence of your own.

26

ephemeral (adj)—momentary; fleeting

When times are difficult, memories of happiness seem **ephemeral.**

Choose a word from the list to complete the following analogy:

ephemeral : lasting :: ethereal : _____

(A) fleeting   (B) mistaken   (C) happy   (D) earthly

Now use *ephemeral* in a sentence of your own.

27

diligent (adj)—hardworking

The rescuers were **diligent** in their efforts to save the museum paintings from the rising floodwaters.

Write synonyms and antonyms in the word web. Add as many circles as you can.

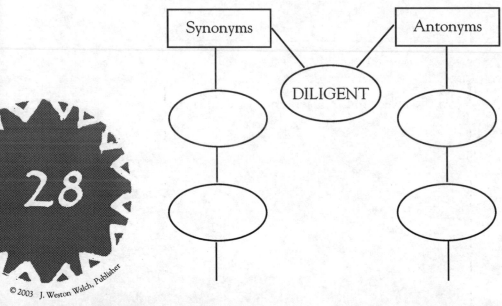

28

abstain (vb)— to refrain from doing something

During training, the player had to **abstain** from eating his favorite foods because he didn't want to gain any extra weight.

_____

Use each of the following forms of *abstain* in a sentence.

abstain (vb) _____

_____

abstinence (n) _____

_____

abstemious (adj) _____

_____

29

© 2003 J. Weston Walch, Publisher

remuneration (n)—payment

I refused to do the boring work asked of me without some form of **remuneration.**

Unscramble the following letters to find synonyms for *remuneration.*

METNAYP   _____

OERCMEPSEN   _____

30

Now use *remuneration* in a sentence of your own.

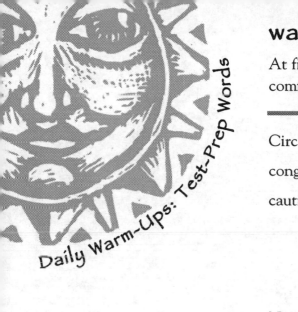

wary (adj)—watchful; alert

At first, the kitten was **wary** of its new home, but soon it grew comfortable and played with its new owners.

Circle the words that are similar in meaning to *wary.*

congruous	careful	cogent	clear
cautious	candid	circumspect	congenial

Now use *wary* in a sentence of your own.

31

subtle (adj)—elusive; sly; ambiguous

The fragrance of the new perfume was so **subtle** that it was difficult to detect its ingredients.

Name three things you could describe using *subtle*.

_____ _____ _____

Write an antonym of *subtle*. _____

32

Now use *subtle* in a sentence of your own.

capricious (adj)—impulsive; unpredictable

The young prince was quite **capricious;** his friends never knew what his next adventure would be.

Circle a synonym for *capricious:*

prepared   whimsical   irresponsible

Circle an antonym for *capricious:*

daring   spontaneous   premeditated

Now use *capricious* in a sentence of your own.

33

amphibious (adj)—able to function both on land and in water

From Greek *amphi* (on both sides) and *bios* (life)

A frog is one example of an **amphibious** creature; it can live on land and in the water.

_____

List another word containing the prefix *amphi–*.

_____

Give three examples of other amphibious creatures.

_____   _____   _____

34

restrained (adj)—controlled; restricted

The angry young man's behavior became **restrained** after several weeks of attending private school.

_____

Complete the following analogy.

restrained : regulated :: intrepid : _____

Now use *restrained* in a sentence of your own.

hackneyed (adj)—overused; clichéd

Although the images and metaphors used in the holiday poem are **hackneyed,** the rhyme is still fun to recite.

Circle each correct answer.

Is *trite* a synonym or an antonym of *hackneyed*?   synonym   antonym

Is *stereotyped* a synonym or an antonym of *hackneyed*?   synonym   antonym

Is *uncommon* a synonym or an antonym of *hackneyed*?   synonym   antonym

Now use *hackneyed* in a sentence of your own.

36

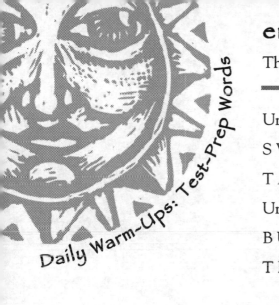

emaciated (adj)—skinny, especially from hunger

The **emaciated** abandoned cat begged for food and milk.

Unscramble the synonyms for *emaciated*.

SWACRYN _____

TANUG _____

Unscramble the antonyms for *emaciated*.

BURTOS _____

THREAY _____

Now use *emaciated* in a sentence of your own.

37

antagonist (n)—opponent

The two senators became bitter **antagonists** when they disagreed on the direction of the state legislation.

Write an antonym for *antagonist*. _____

Now use *antagonist* in a sentence of your own.

38

pretentious (adj)—self-important; pompous

The **pretentious** home and cars gave Gatsby a false sense of importance.

Circle the answer to each question:

If someone were pretentious, would he or she like lavish things?

     yes   no

If someone were pretentious, would he or she frequently be showy?

     yes   no

If someone were pretentious, would he or she be discreet?

     yes   no

Now use *pretentious* in a sentence of your own.

39

intuitive (adj)—instinctive; untaught

My mother's talent with decorating is completely **intuitive;** she's never taken a decorating course.

_____

What is the opposite of *intuitive*? Write it here.

_____

Now write one sentence using both *intuitive* and one of its antonyms.

40

parched (adj)—dried up; thirsty

The **parched** traveler searched everywhere for a drop of water.

Write one synonym for *parched*. _____

Write one antonym for *parched*. _____

Now use *parched* in a sentence of your own.

41

conflagration (n)—a large, destructive fire

After the **conflagration** had finally subsided, those who still had homes returned to them.

Use *conflagration* in a sentence of your own.

Now use the verb form *conflagrate* in a sentence of your own.

disdain (n)—scorn; contempt

Those who did not share the government's beliefs treated the soldiers with **disdain.**

Complete the following analogy.

disdain : contempt :: admiration : _____

Now write your own analogy using *disdain.*

Quiz

Match each word on the left with its definition on the right. Write the letter of the definition on the line next to the vocabulary word.

___ 1. emulate   a. fleeting

___ 2. assiduous   b. fearless

___ 3. prosaic   c. conclude

___ 4. cryptic   d. to become similar

___ 5. ephemeral   e. ordinary

___ 6. pretentious   f. secretive

___ 7. conform   g. to copy

___ 8. infer   h. diligent

___ 9. altercation   i. a noisy dispute

___ 10. intrepid   j. pompous

44

Now write an antonym for each of the following words.

disdain _____   parched _____

wary _____   sagacious _____

insipid (adj)—bland

The restaurant critic claimed that many items on the restaurant's menu were **insipid,** lacking any kind of spice.

Circle the words that are similar in meaning to *insipid*.

tasty   dull   tasteless   pungent   unsavory   savory   seasoned

Now use *insipid* in a sentence of your own.

45

enervate (vb)—to tire; to weaken

The Special Forces team hoped that the night raids would **enervate** the enemy.

Decide whether each word below is a synonym or an antonym of *enervate*. Write each word under the appropriate heading.

revive   energize   lessen   relax   wane   enliven   tire   renew

Synonyms	**Antonyms**

46

Now use *enervate* in a sentence of your own.

covert (adj)—secretive; veiled

The fictitious James Bond was a master of **covert** operations.

_____

Write an antonym for *covert*. _____

Write an analogy using *covert*.

covert : _____ :: _____ : _____

Now use *covert* in a sentence of your own.

47

adulation (n)—high praise

After the spelling bee, the audience lavished the ten-year-old winner with **adulation.**

Think of some synonyms for *adulation*. Write them below.

48

Now use *adulation* in a sentence of your own.

caucus (n)—a closed meeting of members of a political party

The word originates from the Algonquin Indian word *caucauesu* (elder, counselor).

The expression *smoke-filled room* is another term for *caucus*, a meeting of politicians. It has been explained that this term was used not only because politicians may smoke as they discuss the issues, but many of the issues are likely to be cloudy as a result of all the "hot air."

The president met with the delegated **caucus** to discuss the response to terrorist threats.

___

Use *caucus* in a sentence of your own.

49

indignant (adj)—angry; offended

The elderly passenger was **indignant** when the security officer examined her luggage.

Complete the following analogy.

indignant : composed :: incensed : _____

50

Now use *indignant* in a sentence of your own.

deleterious (adj)—harmful

The **deleterious** effects of the new drug continued long after the patients stopped using it.

Circle the synonyms and draw a line under the antonyms of *deleterious*.

destructive   detrimental   beneficial   injurious   harmless   safe

Now use *deleterious* in a sentence of your own.

51

© 2003 J. Weston Walch, Publisher

ostentatious (adj)—marked by conspicuous or pretentious display

The mansion built in Newport, Rhode Island, by a millionaire was considered by many to be an **ostentatious** display of wealth.

List three things you would classify as ostentatious displays of wealth.

_____

_____

Now use *ostentatious* in a sentence of your own.

52

scrupulous (adj)—cautious in action; careful

The researcher was **scrupulous** in documenting her sources so that others would receive credit for their ideas.

_____

Write a synonym of *scrupulous*. _____

Write an antonym of *scrupulous*. _____

Now use *scrupulous* in a sentence of your own.

53

prudent (adj)—careful; cautious

Considering their limited funds, the couple decided it would not be **prudent** to purchase a home at this time.

Circle the word that best completes the analogy.

prudent : foolish :: pugnacious : _____

childish   spoiled   peaceful   reactionary

54

Now use *prudent* in a sentence of your own.

querulous (adj)—irritable

The **querulous** old man was a habitual complainer who was never satisfied with his workers.

_____

Write two analogies using *querulous*.

_____ : _____ :: _____ : _____

_____ : _____ :: _____ : _____

Now use *querulous* in a sentence of your own.

55

mundane (adj)—ordinary; common

The **mundane** concerns of day-to-day life occupied Jon's thoughts, whereas his sister's interest was in unusual, extraordinary events.

Write three synonyms for *mundane*.

_____   _____   _____

Now use *mundane* in a sentence of your own.

56

novice (n)—beginner

Although Patrick is a **novice** at skiing, he shows great potential.

Unscramble the following synonym for *novice*.

PARPTENCIE _____

Unscramble the following antonym for *novice*.

TEXPRE _____

Now write one sentence using both *novice* and one of its antonyms.

57

adversity (n)—misfortune

The girl endured much **adversity** in her young life but was able to overcome many obstacles and find success in her writing.

Circle the ten words in the puzzle that are synonyms for *adversity*.

```
N N Q Y T Q E N R Y T P T H V
D I F F I C U L T Y V A R L J
X G T H A R D S H I P G O A O
H G I E W I U O D N S M U R T
R S N N W S O O K E T M B P G
A S C I S I M M I S R N L E R
I C I M I S F O R T U N E N J
N G L P O S O B O G G S J K E
Q S S E L M N S H N G D B F L
T S I D O B E T T S L R E N K
D D H I N D R A N C E O R D
Y M A M S V K C L W N H T P P
X Z M E A L C L L Y Y O T O W
J H K N L C H E D Q Z N M K U
D I S T R E S S N Z B C C J K
```

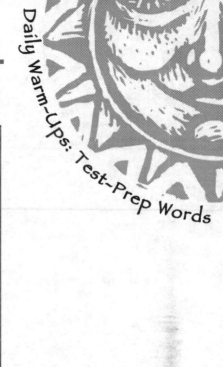

58

compassion (n)—sympathy; mercy

The city of New York showed great **compassion** to the victims' families, helping them both financially and emotionally.

Write a sentence for each of the following forms of *compassion*.

compassion (n) _____

_____

compassionate (adj) _____

_____

compassionately (adv) _____

_____

59

arid (adj)—extremely dry

During the dust storms of the 1930s, the **arid** land produced no crops and many families were forced to abandon their farms.

Circle the synonyms and underline the antonyms of *arid*.

barren moist parched baked damp sodden drenched dehydrated

Now use *arid* in a sentence of your own.

60

integrity (n)—honesty; decency

The new president's **integrity** was a refreshing contrast to the dishonesty of his predecessor, who was convicted of fraud.

List three synonyms for *integrity*.

_____ _____ _____

Now use *integrity* in a sentence of your own.

61

deciduous (adj)—losing leaves in the fall; short-lived

A favorite **deciduous** tree is the maple because of the vibrantly colored leaves it sheds in the fall.

Can you name two deciduous trees?

_____ _____

Now use *deciduous* in a sentence of your own.

62

hypothesis (n)—a theory requiring proof

The professor has an interesting **hypothesis** about the origin of the disease, but there is still no proof to support it.

Write a sentence for each of the following forms of *hypothesis*.

hypothesis (n) _____

_____

hypothesize (vb) _____

_____

hypothetical (adj) _____

_____

63

empathy (n)—sharing of feelings

The root *path* means "feel" or "suffer."

After having suffered as a child, one of Kathryn's greatest strengths as an adult was her **empathy** for others.

_____

Write three other words with the root *path*.

_____   _____   _____

Now use *empathy* in a sentence of your own.

64

scrutinize (vb)—to observe carefully

The archaeologist **scrutinized** the ancient burial site before beginning the expensive digging process.

Complete the analogy.

scan : scrutinize :: look : _____

ponder   stare   regress   meddle   parry

Now use *scrutinize* in a sentence of your own.

65

perfidious (adj)—disloyal

The candidate's **perfidious** advisor revealed all of his boss's secret strategies to the reporter.

Circle the synonyms and underline the antonyms of *perfidious*.

faithless   loyal   faithful   honest

deceitful   corrupt   untrustworthy   dishonorable

Now use *perfidious* in a sentence of your own.

66

orator (n)—speaker

Patrick Henry was a great **orator,** and his "Give Me Liberty" speech will forever be remembered.

_____

List three other great orators.

_____

_____

_____

Now use _orator_ in a sentence of your own.

67

reclusive (adj)—withdrawn; hermitlike

The **reclusive** tendencies of the billionaire caused him to abandon his city life and move to an isolated area of the country.

What occupations might not be appropriate for a reclusive person? List some here.

Write a synonym for *reclusive*.

Write a definition for *recluse*.

Now write one sentence each for the words *recluse* and *reclusive*.

68

transitory (adj)—of brief duration; fleeting

Most of our relationships with neighbors are **transitory**, because we move so frequently.

Unscramble a synonym for *transitory*.

METRORPAY _____

Unscramble an antonym for *transitory*.

TAMPRENEN _____

Now use *transitory* in a sentence of your own.

lineage (n)—ancestry

Many people visit Ellis Island and take the opportunity to trace their **lineage.**

List two synonyms for *lineage*.

_____   _____

Have any members of your family ever traced their lineage? If yes, explain. If no, explain how you might go about it.

70

Now use *lineage* in a sentence of your own.

exasperation (n)—irritation; frustration

The choreographer couldn't hide her **exasperation** when the dancers made a mess of the dance routine.

Circle the words that are similar in meaning to *exasperation*.

annoyance   happiness   disappointment   exuberance

alienation   vexation   advocacy   displeasure

ecstasy   discontent

Now write two antonyms for *exasperation*.

_____   _____

Now use *exasperation* in a sentence of your own.

71

inconsequential (adj)—trivial; unimportant

The manager dismissed the concerns of the employees as **inconsequential** and decided to continue with his current operating plans.

Circle the eight words in the puzzle that are antonyms for *inconsequential.*

```
S W D N E M G B R V D Y Y K
C R I T I C A L J J I E A O
G I E W S H O D N E M T R T
S N N W B I O K E G M E A G
S C O N S E Q U E N T I A L
W R M C U F P B G E A M N J
O U D L Z Q T O G I S P K E
S C R L M N R H N C D O K R
S I G N I F I C A N T R I N
D A V S Y S Q L S J T T R D
M L M P O T S P R I M A R Y
Z R C A L C S L Y Y O N C W
H K R L C H V D Q Z N T K U
```

72

amicable (adj)—agreeable

One of the positive features of the small classrooms was the **amicable** working relationship between teachers and students.

_____

Write three synonyms for *amicable*.

_____   _____   _____

Write three antonyms for *amicable*.

_____   _____   _____

Now use *amicable* and one of its antonyms in the same sentence.

73

collaborate (vb)—to work together

The two authors decided to **collaborate** on the book because they each had expertise in different areas of the subject.

Use each form of *collaborate* below in a sentence of your own.

collaborate (vb) _____

_____

collaboration (n) _____

_____

collaborative (adj) _____

_____

collaborator (n) _____

_____

74

digression (n)—a straying from the main point

The instructor's recounting of his war experience was an interesting **digression** from the history lecture.

_____

Use each form of *digression* below in a sentence of your own.

digress (vb)_____

_____

digression (n) _____

_____

digressionary (adj) _____

_____

75

prosperity (n)—wealth; success

In the post-war years, the country enjoyed great **prosperity,** which was a welcome change from the pre-war Great Depression years.

Complete the following analogy.

success : prosperity :: failure : _____

Now use *prosperity* in a sentence of your own.

76

nefarious (adj)—evil; vicious

The attorney was known for using **nefarious** tactics; she seemed to enjoy her negative reputation.

Circle the synonyms and underline the antonyms of *nefarious*.

mean   benevolent   wicked   impious   virtuous

good   vile   malevolent   upright

Now use *nefarious* in a sentence of your own.

77

formidable (adj)—causing fear or dread

From Latin *formidare* (to fear)

The word can also refer to things that are large or superior, such as formidable accomplishments.

The soldiers fighting the guerilla war turned out to be a **formidable** enemy.

Unscramble the synonyms for *formidable*.

REFSMAOE   _____

SEWOMAE   _____

SREMIPIESV   _____

TUSANTDNGOI   _____

78

Now use *formidable* in a sentence of your own. Be sure to include context clues, and underline those clues in the sentence.

fervid (adj)—passionate; intense

The fans of the championship soccer team were particularly **fervid,** doing everything they could to catch a glimpse of their heroes.

Complete the following analogy.

fervid : zealous :: fetid : _____

Now use *fervid* in a sentence of your own.

79

submissive (adj)—tending to be meek

The **submissive** students quieted as soon as the teacher walked into the room.

Choose a word to complete the following analogy.

strident : noisy :: submissive : _____

energetic   feisty   docile   patient

Now use *submissive* in a sentence of your own.

80

placate (vb)—to soothe; to pacify

The father tried to **placate** the hungry child by offering him candy and cookies.

Write a short paragraph describing a situation in which you tried to placate someone or something.

81

vindicate (vb)—to clear from blame

Marie felt **vindicated** when her dire predictions about the coming flood came true.

Write one sentence using the verb form *vindicated* and one sentence using the noun form *vindication*. Be sure to include context clues in your sentences.

82

prolific (adj)—productive; fertile

Tom Clancy, a **prolific** writer, seems to produce a bestseller every year!

_____

List two antonyms for *prolific*.

_____   _____

Now use *prolific* in a sentence of your own.

83

chastise (vb)—to punish; to discipline

The museum director **chastised** the patron for breaking the valuable vase.

Circle the synonyms for *chastise*.

purify	scold	praise	criticize	exult
reprove	admonish	commend	extol	approve

Now use *chastise* in a sentence of your own.

84

resilient (adj)—quick to recover

Fortunately, Kevin was a **resilient** person and was able to find another job after he was laid off.

_____

Use each form of _resilient_ below in a sentence of your own.

resilient (adj) _____

_____

resiliency (n) _____

_____

resiliently (adv) _____

_____

85

haughty (adj)—arrogant; condescending

Her classmates resented the **haughty** attitude of the new student.

Unscramble a synonym and an antonym for *haughty*.

DOPUR _____

BELHMU _____

Now use *haughty* and one of its antonyms in the same sentence.

86

labyrinth (n)—a maze

When the young woman first arrived in New York, she asked her work colleagues to guide her through the labyrinth of the city.

Circle the synonyms for *labyrinthine*, the adjective form of *labyrinth*.

intricate   simple   circuitous   winding   linear

There is a Greek myth that tells of King Minos placing the Minotaur in a labyrinth. Can you give an example of another famous labyrinth? Write it here.

87

superficial (adj)—lacking in depth

When we met the political candidate, we thought his remarks were **superficial;** he didn't seem to care about our issues.

How is *superficial* used in the above example?

Now use *superficial* in a sentence of your own.

88

Quiz

Match each word on the left with its antonym on the right. Write the letter of the antonym on the line next to the vocabulary word.

_____ 1. insipid   a. amiable

_____ 2. deleterious   b. uncommon

_____ 3. novice   c. poverty

_____ 4. querulous   d. loyal

_____ 5. perfidious   e. savory

_____ 6. covert   f. expert

_____ 7. mundane   g. damp

_____ 8. prosperity   h. kind

_____ 9. arid   i. helpful

____ 10. nefarious   j. open

Now write a synonym for each of the following words.

fervid _____   haughty _____

chastise _____   adulation _____

89

anecdote (n)—a short account of an event

Sitting around the campfire, the leaders entertained the scouts with **anecdotes** of other trips.

Write a personal anecdote below.

90

circuitous (adj)—indirect; roundabout

The taxi driver took a **circuitous** route through the city to avoid rush-hour traffic on the main streets.

Write an antonym for *circuitous*. _____

Now use *circuitous* in a sentence of your own.

augment (vb)—to expand; to make larger

The writer **augmented** his royalty earnings with speaking engagements at bookstores.

Circle the ten words in the puzzle that are synonyms for *augment*.

```
N G R S U P P L E M E N T M E G G
M A F S C I S O I N C R E A S E R
B R O A D E N U R P B G E A I X T
Q V N G T N O S O T O W I S L P I
E I Q S S L L M A G N I F Y O A C
B S T C E A O B M N T D D Y O N T
N S D D J R S Y P Q L E J E L D H
D A Y M A G S V L L E N H A N C E
W M I N T E N S I F Y Y Y O Y O W
X R J H K R L C F V D Q Z N M K U
K Z G M T F X N Y L Z T S V H H G
```

92

citadel (n)—a fortress

The **citadel** was located high on a cliff overlooking the city's harbor.

Unscramble a synonym for *citadel*.

G O D L O T S H R N _____

Words are sometimes used figuratively. That is, they are not used in their literal sense, but rather give the reader an image.

Tell what the "citadels" in the following sentence might be: The ancient green citadels on the hillside protected the valley below from avalanches.

Now use *citadel* in a sentence of your own.

93

fortuitous (adj)—lucky

The trader's timing was **fortuitous;** he cashed out his stock right before the market crashed.

___

Write two synonyms for *fortuitous*.

_____ _____

Write two antonyms for *fortuitous*.

_____ _____

94

Now use *fortuitous* in a sentence of your own.

abhor (vb)—to dislike intensely

Jeffrey **abhorred** the winter weather, so he decided to move from Chicago to Florida.

Circle the synonyms and underline the antonyms of *abhor*.

hate	detest	admire	adore
revere	loathe	esteem	despise

Now use *abhor* in a sentence of your own.

95

curtail (vb)—to shorten; to reduce

When Deb sprained her ankle, she had to **curtail** all physical activity for two weeks.

Complete the following analogy.

CURTAIL : EXTEND ::

(A) settle : arbitrate
(B) debase : degrade
(C) expedite : obstruct
(D) commend : applaud

Now use *curtail* in a sentence of your own.

discredit (vb)— to dishonor; to disgrace

The prosecutor worked hard to **discredit** the eyewitness's testimony, but the jury ultimately believed the defense.

The prefix *dis-* means "to do the opposite of." Write a definition of *discredit* that includes the prefix definition.

Now use *discredit* in a sentence of your own.

97

eclectic (adj)—selecting from various sources

The furnishings that the couple chose for their new apartment were an **eclectic** mix of traditional and modern.

Describe the clothing or furnishings of a person who has an eclectic style.

98

procrastinate (vb)—to delay unnecessarily

The teacher urged us not to **procrastinate;** we should do our homework as soon as we get home.

Write an antonym for *procrastinate*. _____

Use each form of *procrastinate* below in a sentence of your own.

procrastinate (vb) _____

_____

procrastinator (n) _____

_____

99

garrulous (adj)—talkative

The **garrulous** interviewer barely let his guest speak; he just kept firing questions at her until the interview ended.

Unscramble two synonyms for *garrulous*.

T A C H T Y   _____

B O V R E S E   _____

Unscramble two antonyms for *garrulous*.

T I E Q U   _____

V S R E E D E R   _____

Now use *garrulous* in a sentence of your own.

100

Daily Warm-Ups: Test-Prep Words

austere (adj)—stern; unadorned

The lack of decoration made the newly constructed church seem **austere.**

Write an antonym for *austere.* _____

Now use *austere* in a sentence of your own.

catalyst (n)—something causing change

The repression of religious freedom was the **catalyst** that brought many early settlers to America.

What might have been a catalyst of the Civil War?

102

Now use *catalyst* in a sentence of your own.

obstinate (adj)—stubborn

He was an **obstinate** little boy, adamantly refusing to eat any vegetables.

Circle the synonyms and underline the antonyms of *obstinate*.

headstrong   yielding   inflexible   intractable   pliant   submissive

Now use *obstinate* in a sentence of your own.

103

longevity (n)—long life

A recent study of **longevity** revealed that exercising every day contributes to a longer life.

_____

Name three historical figures who enjoyed longevity.

_____

_____

_____

Now use *longevity* in a sentence of your own.

104

jubilation (n)—joy; exultation

After the Brazilian soccer team won the World Cup, the crowd expressed their **jubilation** with cheers.

Use each form of *jubilation* below in a sentence of your own.

jubilation (n) _____

_____

jubilant (adj) _____

_____

105

surreptitious (adj)—characterized by secrecy

The king was unaware of the many **surreptitious** plots being planned by members of his court.

_____

Unscramble two synonyms for *surreptitious*.

ANCLDSENTIE _____

DERNVOCRUE _____

Write one antonym for *surreptitious*. _____

Now use *surreptitious* in a sentence of your own.

106

tenacious (adj)—persistent; resolute

After years of physical therapy, the **tenacious** polio victim eventually walked again.

Write two synonyms for *tenacious*.

_____   _____

Now use *tenacious* in a sentence of your own.

107

pacify (vb)—to restore calm; to bring peace

The mayor made a futile attempt to **pacify** the angry protestors, but he could not settle their differences.

Write a definition for each word form below and use the word in a sentence of your own.

pacifist (n) _____

_____

pacific (adj) _____

_____

pacify (vb) _____

_____

108

bellicose (adj)—warlike; quarrelsome

Soon after conquering the small nation, the **bellicose** leader declared war on another country.

Circle the synonyms and underline the antonyms for the word *bellicose*.

peaceable   meek   aggressive   feisty   combative

Name two people in history who might be described as bellicose.

109

embellish (vb)—to decorate; to add ornamentation

Every time my grandfather tells the story of the accident, he **embellishes** it with more details about his injuries.

Unscramble the three synonyms for *embellish*.

HECENAN   _____

LETAORBAE   _____

MAFPLIY   _____

110

Now use *embellish* in a sentence of your own.

germinate (vb)—to begin to grow

The word is related to the word *germ*, as in "the germ of an idea."

The students were excited to hear that only two weeks after planting, the seeds would **germinate.**

_____

Write a synonym for *germinate*. _____

Now use *germinate* in a sentence of your own.

111

holocaust (n)—widespread destruction, usually by fire

From Greek *holos* (whole) and *kaustos* (burned)

Holocaust is now often used to refer to the Nazi attempt to annihilate the Jews.

Millions of lives were taken in the Nazi **Holocaust.**

Can you think of other words beginning with *holo–* (or its variation, *holi–*)? Write them here.

112

Now use *holocaust* in a sentence of your own.

arcane (adj)—secret; mysterious

The **arcane** rituals and beliefs of the tribe were passed down from generation to generation.

Circle the ten words in the puzzle that are synonyms for *arcane*.

```
C X G T N T S S L G J J G E A O F I
T H G U N K N O W A B L E E R T R G
G R S N N W B M Y S T I F Y I N G A
A F T C S E C R E T S T N V E R W N
E I R I M C X R P B G E H I D D E N
V N A T O O S P T O G I S E K E P I
I Q N I N E X P L I C A B L E L N C
S T G E P O B E N A Y D Y E I N U T
S D E J V S Y S Q L I J E D R D I H
P U Z Z L I N G L L W N H R P P N V
M X Z M C A O B S C U R E Y O W B A
R V E I L E D H V D Q Z N D K U K T
```

113

© 2003 J. Weston Walch, Publisher

egregious (adj)—conspicuously bad

The algebra textbook contained several **egregious** errors, so it was pulled from school shelves.

What would be an egregious error in an English book? A science book?

Now use *egregious* in a sentence of your own.

114

tortuous (adj)—winding; twisting; devious

It was difficult for the jury to follow the **tortuous** path of the conspiracy that unfolded in the courtroom.

Unscramble two synonyms for *tortuous*.

RUICTOCUSI _____

DOKOCER _____

Unscramble two antonyms for *tortuous*.

TAGHSRIT _____

SWREVNUGIN _____

Now use *tortuous* in a sentence of your own.

115

precarious (adj)—uncertain; dependent on chance

The mountain climber lost her **precarious** grip on the face of the cliff and fell 20 feet to the ledge below.

Complete the following analogy.

precarious : secure :: precipitate : _____

Now use *precarious* in a sentence of your own.

116

parochial (adj)—limited in scope

The twins were quite different; Joe's **parochial** ideas were in sharp contrast to Pat's open-mindedness.

Circle the synonyms and underline the antonyms for *parochial*.

provincial   open-minded   cosmopolitan   narrow

restricted   broad-minded

Now use *parochial* in a sentence of your own.

117

© 2003 J. Weston Walch, Publisher

loquacious (adj)—talkative

The students on the debate team were naturally **loquacious,** which often led to long discussions.

Circle each correct answer.

Is *silent* a synonym or an antonym of *loquacious*?   synonym   antonym

Is *verbose* a synonym or an antonym of *loquacious*?   synonym   antonym

Is *reticent* a synonym or an antonym of *loquacious*?   synonym   antonym

Is *garrulous* a synonym or an antonym of *loquacious*?   synonym   antonym

Now use *loquacious* in a sentence of your own.

118

nadir (n)—the lowest point

Nadir refers literally to the lowest point in the heavens, directly opposite the zenith (highest point).

He felt he was at the **nadir** of his career when he lost what had seemed to be an easy case.

List two antonyms for *nadir*.

_____   _____

Now use *nadir* in a sentence of your own.

119

satiated (adj)—fully fed or satisfied

The dictator's desire for power could not be **satiated** until she conquered every country bordering hers.

What kind of appetite is an insatiable appetite?

Now use *satiated* in a sentence of your own.

120

lugubrious (adj)—exaggeratedly mournful

This word can refer to people (a *lugubrious* personality) or to things that make people feel mournful (a *lugubrious* set of circumstances).

The young man wore a **lugubrious** expression for weeks after his favorite musician died.

Circle the antonyms for *lugubrious*.

sad   dismal   blissful   melancholy   merry   cheerful   plaintive

Now use *lugubrious* in a sentence of your own.

121

flamboyant (adj)—ornate; showy

The **flamboyant** carnival costumes lent a festive, exciting air to the Mardi Gras celebration.

Unscramble the synonyms for *flamboyant*.

D I F R O L _____

L A F H Y S _____

Now use *flamboyant* in a sentence of your own.

122

dormant (adj)—sleeping; inactive

The tulip bulbs were **dormant** during the winter, but they came to life and blossomed beautifully in the spring.

List two antonyms for *dormant*.

_____   _____

Is *lethargic* a synonym or an antonym for *dormant*?

_____

Now use *dormant* in a sentence of your own.

123

truncated (adj)—cut off; shortened

The president planned to address the nation for 40 minutes, but he gave a **truncated** speech when an emergency arose.

Circle the synonyms of *truncated*.

extended   curtailed   clipped   augmented   increased   abbreviated

124

Now use *truncated* in a sentence of your own.

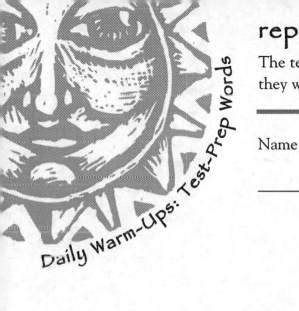

replicate (vb)—to duplicate; to repeat

The team knew that in order to **replicate** last year's winning record, they would have to work very hard.

_____

Name three things that are commonly replicated.

_____   _____   _____

Now use _replicate_ in a sentence of your own.

125

metamorphosis (n)— a transformation; a marked alteration

From Greek *meta* (over) and *morphe* (form)

The students were fascinated by the **metamorphosis** of a tadpole into a frog.

List another example of a metamorphosis.

126

Now use *metamorphosis* in a sentence of your own.

languid (adj)—sluggish; drooping

The **languid** group sat slumped and dozing on the porch, barely noticing the passing neighbors.

Circle the ten words in the puzzle that are antonyms for *languid*.

```
P A E N J R Q V J J C E A
G I N W S A N I M A T E D
S N L O P O O V E G M E S
S V I S R B M A B H E I P
W I V C I R L C G E N I I
E N E R G E T I C T L Q R
S B N L H N R O T C I O I
A L E R T B N U D H V O T
T C D G L K C S S J E L E
M A M S Y K L L W N L R D
Z A C T I V E L Y Y Y Y O
```

127

circumvent (vb)—to avoid by going around; to encircle

From Latin *circum* (around) and *venire* (to come)

The fans figured out a way to **circumvent** security and slipped backstage.

Think of another term that uses the prefix *circum-*. Write it here.

Now use *circumvent* in a sentence of your own.

128

gregarious (adj)—social; liking companionship

Jennifer is an extremely **gregarious** person who spends most of her free time attending parties and other social events.

Complete the following analogy.

GREGARIOUS : LONER ::

(A) angry : competitor

(B) fearful : leader

(C) cautious : player

(D) sociable : hermit

Now use *gregarious* in a sentence of your own.

129

taciturn (adj)—silent; not talkative

Taciturn is related to the musical term *tacet*, which refers to a section of a composition in which a musician does not play.

The quarterback's **taciturn** nature was in sharp contrast to the chattiness of the receiver.

Is *loquacious* a synonym or an antonym of *taciturn*?

Now use *taciturn* in a sentence of your own.

130

ostracize (vb)—to exclude from a group; to banish

After making rude comments at several games, Martin was **ostracized** by the team.

Circle the synonyms of *ostracize*.

welcome   exile   exclude   include   accept   expel

Now use *ostracize* in a sentence of your own.

131

soporific (adj)—causing sleep

The biology lecture proved to be so **soporific** that soon I found myself dozing.

List four things you find soporific.

_____   _____

_____   _____

Now use *soporific* in a sentence of your own.

132

amalgam (n)—a mixture of different elements

The word *amalgam* usually refers to metal alloys, particularly mixtures of mercury and other metals.

The new publishing company was an **amalgam** of small publishers that had battled for the same customers.

Write two synonyms for *amalgam*.

_____   _____

List uses for *amalgam* in contexts other than alloys.

133

Quiz

Match each word on the left with its definition on the right. Write the letter of the definition on the line next to the vocabulary word.

___ 1. circuitous	a. lucky
___ 2. arcane	b. sleep-inducing
___ 3. languid	c. fortress
___ 4. citadel	d. talkative
___ 5. gregarious	e. mysterious
___ 6. flamboyant	f. indirect
___ 7. fortuitous	g. shortened
___ 8. soporific	h. ornate
___ 9. truncated	i. sluggish
___ 10. garrulous	j. social

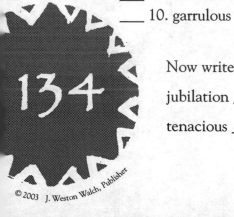

134

Now write an antonym for each of the following words.

jubilation _____   abhor _____

tenacious _____   austere _____

juxtapose (vb)—to place side by side

An interesting element in Asa's artwork is the way he **juxtaposes** colors in unexpected combinations.

Words that contain *pose* often relate to position or placement. Can you think of some other words that contain *pose*? Write them here.

Now use *juxtapose* in a sentence of your own.

135

carnivore (n)—a flesh-eating animal

From Latin *carno* (flesh) and *orare* (devour)

Lions, sharks, and bears are all examples of **carnivores;** they all prey on other animals.

Write another word with the root *car* (flesh).

Now write another word containing *vore*.

Now use *carnivore* in a sentence of your own.

136

plummet (vb)—to fall or plunge straight downward

The skydiver's parachute opened as he **plummeted** toward the target.

Unscramble the following synonyms for *plummet*.

L E P N U G   _____

N E D L I C E   _____

Now use *plummet* in a sentence of your own.

137

expunge (vb)—to strike out; to erase

The editor's goal was to **expunge** all the errors she found on the company's web site.

Circle the synonyms for *expunge*.

incorporate   include   omit   eliminate   prepare

delete   discard   increase   eradicate

Now use *expunge* in a sentence of your own.

138

scintillating (adj)—sparkling

From Latin *scintilla* (spark)

The well-known entertainer was famous for her brilliant wit and **scintillating** conversation.

What word that refers to sparkling strips hung on a Christmas tree

is related to *scintillate*? _____

Unscramble the following synonym for *scintillate*.

KITWENL _____

Now use *scintillating* in a sentence of your own.

139

© 2003 J. Weston Walch, Publisher

cacophony (n)—harsh or discordant sound

The junior high school marching band created a grating **cacophony** as they tried to walk and play at the same time.

Name three sounds that are cacophonous.

_____

_____

_____

Now use *cacophony* in a sentence of your own.

140

disheveled (adj)—untidy

The candidate for the job appeared **disheveled:** Her suit was not pressed, her hair was dirty, and her shoes were scuffed.

Circle the synonyms and underline the antonyms of *disheveled*.

neat   ruffled   tidy   orderly   rumpled   mussed

Now use *disheveled* in a sentence of your own.

141

fecund (adj)—fruitful; productive

From Latin *fecundus* (fruitful)

Fecund can apply to physical things, such as animals that produce lots of offspring and plants that produce lots of fruit. It can also apply to intangible things, such as a fecund mind.

The **fecund** mind of William Shakespeare produced a memorable body of work.

Unscramble the following antonyms of *fecund*.

R E B A R N _____

T I L E R S E _____

142

Now use *fecund* in a sentence of your own.

Daily Warm-Ups: Test-Prep Words

harbinger (n)—a forerunner; a herald

After a long winter in New England, the robin is a **harbinger** of spring.

List three synonyms for *harbinger*.

_____ _____ _____

Explain the following sentence: The Declaration of Independence was the harbinger of independence movements around the world.

Now use *harbinger* in a sentence of your own.

143

timorous (adj)—easily frightened

Bobby was a **timorous** little boy who relied on his older brothers to speak up for him and fight his battles.

Circle four synonyms and six antonyms for *timorous* in the puzzle.

```
F R I G H A T E S C A R
R S S E L R A E F A C S
A F R C A I D B Y T B C
M A L O M R S C O O R A
L F A U N N F O O D A R
A P P R E H E N S I V E
C R E A D A A F Y P E A
P U R G E R R I O E T F
R E B E F M F D U R H R
U N I O Y S U E T T E A
L C P U L W L N O N B I
L E A S E D A T F I L D
A F R I G H T E N E D E
```

144

zealous (adj)—enthusiastically devoted

The **zealous** football fans were rewarded for their loyalty when the New England Patriots won the Super Bowl.

Write appropriate words in the word web below. Add as many circles as you can.

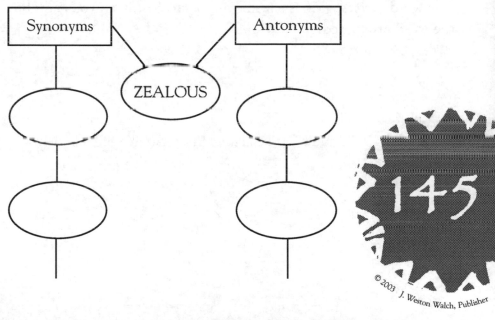

145

bombastic (adj)—<small>pretentious; pompous</small>

The press accused the senator of **bombastic** speech—full of outrageous claims that had no basis in fact.

Name two types of speech or writing that are frequently bombastic.

_____   _____

The word *gobbledygook* is a synonym for *bombast*. Can you guess how the word originated?

Now use *bombastic* in a sentence of your own.

146

effervescent (adj)—bubbly; lively

Kate's **effervescent** personality made her the perfect choice for her dream profession: hosting a talk show.

Can you name one thing that effervesces in the literal sense of

bubbling? Write it here. _____

Write three synonyms for *effervescent* in reference to people.

_____ _____ _____

Now use *effervescent* in a sentence of your own.

147

pinnacle (n)—the highest point

Winning an Oscar for her performance was the pinnacle of the actress's career.

Unscramble two synonyms for *pinnacle*.

MUMSTI _____

NEZHIT _____

Now use *pinnacle* in a sentence of your own.

148

obdurate (adj)—hard; unmoved by persuasion

Although the doctor warned him against it, the boxer was **obdurate** in his decision to continue fighting.

Write three synonyms for *obdurate*.

_____   _____   _____

Write two physical things that are *obdurate*.

_____   _____

Now use *obdurate* in a sentence of your own.

149

ravenous (adj)—hungry; very eager

After three days of being trapped underground, the coal miners were **ravenous.**

Circle each correct answer.

Is *voracious* a synonym or an antonym of *ravenous*?   synonym   antonym

Is *satiated* a synonym or an antonym of *ravenous*?   synonym   antonym

150

Now use *ravenous* in a sentence of your own in connection with something other than food.

pulchritude (adj)—physical beauty

Helen of Troy was admired for her **pulchritude;** hers was the "face that launched a thousand ships."

Look at the chart. What error do you see? Correct the error.

PULCHRITUDE	
Synonyms	Antonyms
loveliness	ugliness
comeliness	unattractiveness
attractiveness	gorgeousness
beauty	grotesqueness

151

incarcerate (vb)—to put in prison

The cat burglar was to be **incarcerated** for a year, but she was granted parole after three months.

Explain what *incarcerated* means in the following sentence: The young man was incarcerated by his own sense of defeat.

Now use *incarcerate* in a sentence of your own.

152

ludicrous (adj)—laughable because of obvious absurdity

Although the theory presented by the eccentric scientist was **ludicrous,** we listened politely.

Which of these words is a synonym for *ludicrous*? Circle your choice.

lucid   dismal   ridiculous   suspicious

Now use *ludicrous* in a sentence of your own.

153

xenophobia (n)—fear or hatred of strangers or foreigners

From Greek *xenos* (stranger) and *phobia* (fear of)

After the terrorist attacks of 2001, **xenophobia** became more prevalent among Americans, and many people wanted to tighten immigration policies.

List two other words that end in *–phobia* and give their definitions.

Now use *xenophobia* in a sentence of your own.

154

progeny (n)—an offspring; a descendant

The photographic exhibit at Ellis Island showed my great–great–grandparents and all their **progeny.**

Look up *progenitor* in a dictionary. Write its definition here.

The word *kin* is related to the same root as that of *progeny.*
Define *kin.*

Now use *progeny* in a sentence of your own.

155

irascible (adj)—easily angered; hot-tempered

We learned to keep quiet around the **irascible** old man; we knew anything we said would make him angry.

Write appropriate words in the word web. Add as many circles as you can.

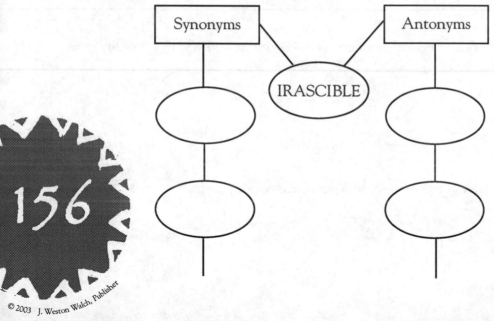

156

cadence (n)—rhythm

The French student spoke with a lovely **cadence;** it was a pleasure listening to her.

Circle what does *not* have cadence.

music   poetry   rowing   the tides   corn popping

Now use *cadence* in a sentence of your own.

157

indolent (adj)—lazy

The word *indolent* can be used to describe a lazy person and also to describe things that encourage laziness, such as the indolent heat of summer.

The employee's **indolent** habits and inability to meet goals cost him his job.

Write two synonyms for *indolent*.

_____   _____

Write two antonyms for *indolent*.

_____   _____

Now use *indolent* in a sentence of your own.

158

pugilist (n)—a fighter; a boxer

From Latin *pugil* (boxer)

Muhammad Ali, the famous **pugilist**, was formerly known as Cassius Clay.

Can you name two other famous pugilists? Write their names here.

_____   _____

Now use *pugilist* in a sentence of your own.

159

recalcitrant (adj)—stubbornly resistant to authority or restraint

The **recalcitrant** kindergartener refused to perform any of the requested tasks; he was as stubborn as a mule!

Look at the chart. What errors do you see? Correct them.

RECALCITRANT	
Synonyms	Antonyms
amenable	docile
stubborn	pliable
pigheaded	flexible
unmanageable	malleable
intractable	defiant

160

luminary (n)—a person of prominence or brilliant achievement

From Latin *lumen* (light)

Lauren's father was a **luminary** in the literary world, and everyone sought his advice on how to become a best-selling author.

List two people in history who might be described as luminaries.

_____   _____

Now use *luminary* in a sentence of your own.

161

ruminate (vb)—to ponder; to think over

Regrettably, I spent too much valuable time during the SAT **ruminating** about problems I couldn't solve.

Circle a word that could replace *ruminate* in the following sentence: How long will it take you and your colleagues to ruminate upon the theory proposed by the geology professor?

reinforce   articulate   reflect   depend

Now use *ruminate* in a sentence of your own.

pejorative (adj)—having bad connotations; disparaging

The teacher scolded Ashley for the **pejorative** remarks she made about her classmate's history report.

Write one synonym for *pejorative*. _____

Write one antonym for *pejorative*. _____

Now use *pejorative* in a sentence of your own.

163

buffoon (n)—a clown; a laughable person

From Italian *buffa* (joke, jest)

The twins were very different; one was always serious and the other was known as the school **buffoon.**

Write two synonyms for *buffoon*.

_____   _____

Now use *buffoon* in a sentence of your own.

164

dulcet (adj)—sweet; melodious; soothing

From Latin *dulcis* (sweet)

Dulcet can refer to things sweet to the taste, things soothing to the ear, or things generally agreeable, such as dulcet weather.

The **dulcet** tone of the mother's voice lulled the baby to sleep.

Circle an antonym for *dulcet*.   pleasing   offensive

What do you think the phrase *dolce vita* means?

Now use *dulcet* in a sentence of your own.

165

ebullient (adj)—overflowing with enthusiasm or excitement

The children became so **ebullient** during the holiday party that the teacher had to ask for five minutes of silence.

Write appropriate words in the word web. Add as many circles as you can.

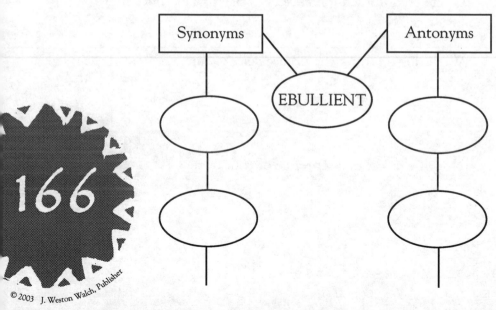

166

lethargy (n)—lack of energy; abnormal drowsiness

My parents say I'm famous for my **lethargy** because all I do is sit on the couch all day.

Circle the word that properly characterizes someone who is lethargic.

energetic   resilient   wistful   exuberant   sluggish

Now use *lethargy* in a sentence of your own.

167

indigenous (adj)—existing naturally in a particular environment or region

The koala bear is a small marsupial that is **indigenous** to Australia.

Name a plant that is indigenous to your area.

Now use *indigenous* in a sentence of your own.

168

erudite (adj)—very learned

Geoff's father was an **erudite** scholar; he had read almost everything printed about Shakespeare.

Unscramble a synonym for *erudite*.

L A S C H R O L Y _____

Unscramble an antonym for *erudite*.

G N A R T I O N _____

Now use *erudite* in a sentence of your own.

169

incongruous (adj)—not compatible or harmonious; out of place

The frilly party dress seemed **incongruous** in the closet filled with jeans and sweatshirts.

Circle the word that is an antonym of *incongruous*.

disagreeing   unsuitable   elegant   harmonious   irrelevant

Now use *incongruous* in a sentence of your own.

170

vociferous (adj)—loud or vehement; noisy

The baseball commissioner continued his speech despite the **vociferous** protests of the players and fans.

Number the following words to show a logical increase in degree.

_____ noisy

_____ muffled

_____ vociferous

_____ silent

Now use *vociferous* in a sentence of your own.

171

© 2003 J. Weston Walch, Publisher

reticent (adj)—not speaking freely; reserved

Maria was at first **reticent** about speaking at meetings, but soon she opened up and offered her valuable opinions.

Circle the synonyms and underline the antonyms of *reticent*.

silent   expressive   open   quiet   talkative

outgoing   uncommunicative

Now use *reticent* in a sentence of your own.

172

meticulous (adj)—extremely careful and precise

The artist had to be **meticulous** as he assembled the ship's model.

Which occupation would most likely require someone to be meticulous?

chauffer   ball player   farmer   proofreader   actor

Write an antonym for *meticulous.* _____

Now use *meticulous* in a sentence of your own.

173

obliterate (vb)—to destroy; to leave no trace

The small beachfront community was **obliterated** by a tidal wave.

Complete the following analogy.

obliterate : destroy :: cherish : _____

hate   harm   love   deride

Now use *obliterate* in a sentence of your own.

174

innocuous (adj)—not harmful or injurious

A few spiders are poisonous, but most are **innocuous** and pose no danger.

Write one synonym for *innocuous.* _____

Complete the word web below.

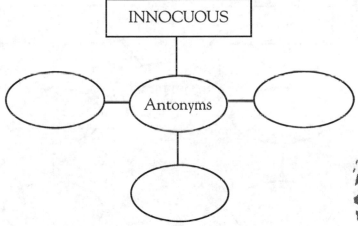

INNOCUOUS

Antonyms

Now use *innocuous* in a sentence of your own.

175

propitious (adj)—favorable

January was not the most **propitious** time to advertise our holiday pumpkin pies.

Write appropriate words in the word web. Add as many circles as you can.

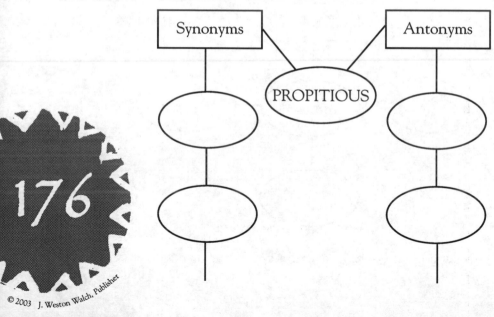

176

veracity (n)—truthfulness; accuracy

The congressman had a reputation for **veracity,** so everyone believed his campaign statements.

How many words can you think of that are related in some way to the word *veracity*?

Create a word web showing the relationships between these words and *veracity*.

177

prodigal (adj)—carelessly or recklessly extravagant; wasteful

The **prodigal** son soon wasted his inheritance on a lavish lifestyle.

Name three stories or films in which a prodigal son is featured.

_____

_____

_____

Now use _prodigal_ in a sentence of your own.

178

magnanimous (adj)—showing courageous spirit, especially in forgiving insult or injury; not selfish

After watching the World War II documentary, we could appreciate the **magnanimous** suffering of the Battle of the Bulge soldiers.

Circle the word that does not belong with the others. Tell why it does not belong.

magnanimous   brave   courageous   fearful   intrepid   valiant

Now use *magnanimous* in a sentence of your own.

179

Quiz

Match each word on the left with its antonym on the right. Write the letter of the antonym on the line next to the vocabulary word.

____ 1. disheveled   a. barren

____ 2. indolent   b. dishonesty

____ 3. scintillating   c. dull

____ 4. pinnacle   d. energetic

____ 5. fecund   e. negligent

____ 6. vociferous   f. tidy

____ 7. meticulous   g. harmful

____ 8. veracity   h. nadir

____ 9. propitious   i. unfavorable

____ 10. innocuous   j. quiet

Now write a synonym for each of the following words.

expunge _____   ravenous _____

irascible _____   obliterate _____

180

In all cases, students' original sentences and lists will vary.

1. possible synonyms: dispute, controversy, squabble, strife, fracas, melee, brawl
2. possible antonyms: impoverished, lean, poverty-stricken
3. occult
4. possible synonyms: misadventure, misstep, defeat
5. diurnal
6. possible examples: one's mind, one's interest, knives and tools, anger
7. possible synonyms: brave, courageous, dauntless, daring; possible antonyms: timid, fearful, shy, bashful, apprehensive
8. possible *demo-* words: democracy, demography
9. synonyms: extra, inessential, wasteful, extravagant, surplus; antonyms: bare, necessary, minimal, sparse, scanty
10. C
11. possible synonyms: persistent, industrious, earnest
12. C; D
13. D
14. synonyms: fraudulent, phony, affected; antonyms: valid, factual, genuine
15. D; possible antonyms: uneducated, slow, dull
16. to draw reasonable conclusions from the context of the reading
17. possible antonyms: uncertain, preventable
18. Definitions will vary.
19. lengthen
20. possible synonyms: cool, snobby, haughty; possible antonym: praising
21. C
22. possible synonyms: enmity, ill-will; possible antonyms: affection, fondness
23. Anwers will vary.
24. possible antonyms: extraordinary, exceptional, scintillating
25. Answers will vary.
26. witless
27. D
28. possible synonyms: earnest, careful, attentive, alert; possible antonyms: careless, lazy, neglectful, reckless
29. Answers will vary.
30. payment; recompense

Daily Warm-Ups: Test-Prep Words

31. careful, cautious, circumspect
32. possible antonyms: obvious, glaring, clear, showy
33. whimsical; premeditated
34. possible answer: amphitheater; possible amphibians: toads, salamanders
35. possibilities: brave, undaunted, fearless
36. synonym; synonym; antonym
37. scrawny, gaunt; robust, hearty
38. possible antonyms: friend, supporter, advocate
39. yes; yes; no
40. possible answers: learned, taught
41. possible synonym: thirsty; possible antonyms: satisfied, moist
42. Answers will vary.
43. possibilities: adulation, respect
44. 1. g, 2. h, 3. e, 4. f, 5. a, 6. j, 7. d, 8. c, 9. i, 10. b
45. dull, tasteless, unsavory
46. synonyms: lessen, relax, wane, tire; antonyms: revive, energize, enliven, renew
47. possible antonyms: overt, open; Analogies will vary.

48. possible synonyms: approval, appreciation, applause, regard
49. Sentences will vary.
50. possibilities: collected, amiable
51. synonyms: destructive, detrimental, injurious; antonyms: beneficial, harmless, safe
52. Answers will vary.
53. possible synonyms: painstaking, exact; possible antonyms: careless, haphazard
54. peaceful
55. Answers will vary.
56. possible synonyms: normal, ordinary, everyday
57. apprentice; expert
58. misfortune, hardship, obstacle, distress, impediment, trouble, struggle, difficulty, hindrance, crisis
59. Sentences will vary.
60. synonyms: barren, parched, baked, dehydrated; antonyms: moist, damp, sodden, drenched
61. possible synonyms: truthfulness, honor, trustworthiness
62. some deciduous trees: oak, elm, maple, birch
63. Sentences will vary.

64. possibilities: sympathy, apathy, pathos
65. stare
66. synonyms: faithless, deceitful, corrupt, untrustworthy, dishonorable; antonyms: loyal, faithful, honest
67. Answers will vary.
68. possibilities: politician, lecturer, trial lawyer, salesperson; possible synonyms: withdrawn, solitary; Definitions will vary.
69. temporary; permanent
70. possible synonyms: background, heritage; Answers will vary.
71. synonyms: annoyance, disappointment, vexation, displeasure, discontent; possible antonyms: contentment, pleasure
72. consequential, chief, important, critical, significant, vital, crucial, primary
73. possible synonyms: friendly, pleasant, genial; possible antonyms: unfriendly, antagonistic, contrary
74. Sentences will vary.
75. Sentences will vary.
76. possibilities: impoverishment, poverty

77. synonyms: mean, wicked, impious, vile, malevolent; antonyms: benevolent, virtuous, good, upright
78. fearsome, awesome, impressive, outstanding
79. possibilities: smelly, foul
80. docile
81. Paragraphs will vary.
82. Sentences will vary.
83. possible antonyms: unproductive, barren
84. scold, criticize, reprove, admonish
85. Sentences will vary.
86. proud; humble
87. intricate, circuitous, winding; Examples will vary.
88. Answers will vary.
89. 1. e, 2. i, 3. f, 4. a, 5. d, 6. j, 7. b, 8. c, 9. g, 10. h
90. Anecdotes will vary.
91. possible antonyms: direct, straight
92. widen, enlarge, increase, broaden, magnify, enhance, expand, amplify, intensify, supplement
93. stronghold; citadels = trees
94. possible synonyms: fortunate, lucky; possible antonyms: unfortunate, unlucky

Daily Warm-Ups: Test-Prep Words

95. synonyms: hate, detest, loathe, despise; antonyms: admire, adore, revere, esteem
96. C
97. Definitions will vary.
98. Descriptions will vary.
99. possible antonym: hasten; Sentences will vary.
100. chatty, verbose; quiet, reserved
101. possible antonyms: adorned, decorated, spare
102. Answers will vary.
103. synonyms: headstrong, inflexible, intractable; antonyms: yielding, pliant, submissive
104. Answers will vary.
105. Sentences will vary.
106. clandestine, undercover; possible antonyms: open, bold, public
107. possible synonyms: determined, resolute
108. Answers will vary.
109. synonyms: aggressive, feisty, combative; antonyms: peaceable, meek
110. enhance, elaborate, amplify
111. possible synonym: sprout
112. holistic, holograph, catholic, hologram

113. inexplicable, unexplained, veiled, secret, obscure, strange, mystifying, hidden, puzzling, unknowable
114. Answers will vary.
115. circuitous, crooked; straight, unswerving
116. possibilities: premeditated, expected
117. synonyms: provincial, narrow, restricted; antonyms: open-minded, cosmopolitan, broad-minded
118. antonym; synonym; antonym; synonym
119. possible antonyms: top, apex, summit, zenith, pinnacle, acme
120. Answers will vary.
121. blissful, merry, cheerful
122. florid, flashy
123. possible antonyms: awake, alert, active; synonym
124. curtailed, clipped, abbreviated
125. possibilities: experiments, documents, pictures
126. possible answer: a caterpillar into a butterfly
127. vivacious, lively, blithe, animated, energetic, spirited, alert, active, enlivened, sprightly
128. possibilities: circumnavigate, circumlocution
129. D

130. antonym
131. exile, exclude, expel
132. possible answers: sleeping aids, warm milk, reading, hot weather
133. possible synonyms: combination, union, medley
134. 1. f, 2. e, 3. i, 4. c, 5. j, 6. h, 7. a, 8. b, 9. g, 10. d
135. possibilities: oppose, repose, impose, suppose
136. possibilities: carrion, carnal, carnage; herbivore, omnivore
137. plunge, decline
138. omit, eliminate, delete, discard, eradicate
139. tinsel; twinkle
140. possible answers: crows cawing, wheels screeching, doors squeaking
141. synonyms: ruffled, rumpled, mussed; antonyms: neat, tidy, orderly
142. barren, sterile
143. possible synonyms: precursor, predecessor, forefather; Answers will vary.
144. synonyms: apprehensive, fearful, frightened, afraid; antonyms: fearless, courageous, confident, intrepid, brave, bold

145. possible synonyms: eager, intense, ardent, fanatical, fervid; possible antonyms: detached, indifferent, objective, blasé
146. possible answers: political speeches, advertisements; gobbledygook = a speaker using lots of long words sounds like a turkey gobbling
147. possible answer: soda pop; possible synonyms: animated, exhilarated, exuberant
148. summit, zenith
149. possible synonyms: unfeeling, inflexible, unyielding, unbending; physical things: rock, diamonds
150. synonym, antonym
151. gorgeousness is not an antonym
152. Answers will vary.
153. ridiculous
154. Answers will vary.
155. Answers will vary.
156. possible synonyms: touchy, testy, cranky, cross; possible antonyms: amiable, agreeable, placid, peaceful
157. corn popping

Daily Warm-Ups: Test-Prep Words

158. possible synonyms: idle, shiftless;
     possible antonyms: industrious, diligent
159. Answers will vary.
160. *Amenable* should be in the antonym list;
     defiant should be in the synonym list.
161. Answers will vary.
162. reflect
163. possible synonyms: demeaning, belittling,
     insulting; possible antonyms: approving,
     supportive, encouraging
164. possible synonyms: comic, comedian
165. offensive; *dolce vita* = sweet life
166. possible synonyms: ecstatic, giddy, exuberant,
     exhilarated; possible antonyms: sullen, gloomy,
     apathetic
167. sluggish
168. Answers will vary.
169. scholarly; ignorant

170. harmonious
171. 3, 2, 4, 1
172. synonyms: silent, quiet, uncommunicative;
     antonyms: expressive, open, talkative, outgoing
173. proofreader; possible antonyms: sloppy, careless,
     haphazard, shoddy
174. love
175. synonyms: harmless, benign; possible antonyms:
     injurious, harmful, evil, hurtful, detrimental
176. possible synonyms: approving, agreeable,
     auspicious; possible antonyms: unfavorable,
     inopportune, disadvantageous
177. Answers will vary.
178. Answers will vary.
179. The word *fearful* does not belong with the other
     words because it is an antonym of magnanimous.
180. 1. f, 2. d, 3. c, 4. h, 5. a, 6. j, 7. e, 8. b, 9. i, 10. g

Turn downtime into learning time!

Other books in the

Daily Warm-Ups series:

- Algebra
- Analogies
- Biology
- Critical Thinking
- Earth Science
- Geography
- Geometry
- Journal Writing
- Poetry
- Pre-Algebra
- Shakespeare
- Spelling & Grammar
- U.S. History
- Vocabulary
- Writing
- World History